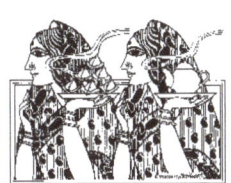

A COLLECTOR'S BOOK
of EIGHT DRAWINGS
with EIGHT INDIAN VEGETARIAN
RECIPES

Presented to

Name

_____

Presented by

Name

_____

_____

Date

_____

This present edition
was inspired by the previous
limited edition of
30 copies for collectors
'A collector's book of
eight delicious drawings
by Biman Mullick,
accompanied by eight
equally delicious recipes
by Aparajita Mullick,'
printed in Great Britain
by Jonathan Doney FSTD at
The Spitfire Press
2016.

The accompanying drawings
are reproduced
with the permission of
BBC/Radio Times.

A Collector's Book of Eight Drawings by Biman Mullick with Eight Indian Vegetarian Recipes by Aparajita Mullick

ISBN 9781794430556

Copyright
Aparajita Mullick 2019

1st International Edition
February 2019

Contacts
Aparajita & Biman Mullick
33 Stillness Road
London SE23 1NG
Phone: +44(0)20 8690 4649
Email:
bimanmullick@lineone.net

Web addresses
http://sites.google.com/site/mullickbiman/
Biman Mullick.com
Biman Mullick | facebook
Biman Mullick | YouTube

Acknowledgements
Shubhasish Kundu,
Antony Mason, Sandra Mullick,
Arthur Soburj Mullick Olver,
Edith Mohima Mullick Olver
and Olga Prothoma Olver
for their Contributions.

All rights reserved.
No part of this publication may be reproduced, stored in a retrieval system or transmitted in any form or by any means, electronic, mechanical, photocopying, recording or otherwise, without the prior permission of the authors.

A few books with a major contribution by Biman:

India and her neighbours
Oxford University Press
ISBN 0 19 910104 3

The Amazing Adventures of Hanuman: BBC
ISBN 056321428-0

Myths and Legends of India
Hamlyn: London
Sun Books: Melbourne
ISBN 0600001296

The Monkeys: Macmillan:
London, Melbourne, Toronto
St Martin's Press: New York

The Most Beautiful Child
Cambridge University Press
ISBN 0521468795

The Man and the Tiger/The Flowers in the River
Harper Collins:
London and Glasgow
ISBN 0003133583

All India
New Burlington Books

The Way of the Hindu
Hulton: UK
ISBN 071750826 8

Towards a Smoke-free Health Service
Cleanair: London
ISBN 0951344624

The Living Arts of India
Arts Council of Great
Britain: London
ISBN 072870323 8

Singing Together
BBC
ISBN 563080418

দুর্গা Durer Durga
A memoir in Bengali
Paperback: ISBN 9781534937987
Hardback: ISBN 9788193833209

My 1st book of Bengali
ISBN 9781539142744

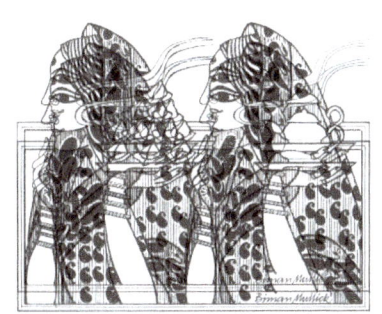

A COLLECTOR'S BOOK of EIGHT DRAWINGS by BIMAN MULLICK with EIGHT INDIAN VEGETARIAN RECIPES by APARAJITA MULLICK

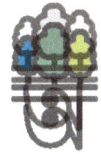

To
my mother Shroddha Devi
who taught me to draw a monkey
from the figure 5 in Bengali.
That was my first experience of drawing.
I filled an exercise book
with little little monkeys.
Biman

To
my mother MadhabiRani Devi
who taught me how to cook.
Aparajita

Contents

A note by Biman Mullick 8

Notes by Aparajita Mullick and Jonathan Doney 9

Tandoori, a tenderising treat 10

Aubergine, a virtuous vegetable 14

Biryani, with a conscience 18

Protein in a pod 22

Charismatic Korma 26

Singara, horns without dilemmas 30

A different ball game 36

A roast to grace your table 40

Contributors 44

I felt highly honoured and deeply moved when one day Jonathan rang me and expressed his desire to produce a limited-edition book based on my drawings, which would be a collector's item. I have known Jonathan since the early 70s, when I was a visiting lecturer in graphic design at Harlow Technical College and he was one of my students. As a so-called teacher I did not 'teach', I merely shared my love, interest and enthusiasm for the subject. I was lucky enough to have students like Jonathan; some of them made a successful career in the field of visual communications.

Jonathan proposed to use a set of eight drawings which I had produced for the BBC and published in Radio Times accompanying recipes by Madhur Jaffrey.

My drawings were not so-called illustrations: they were drawings loosely connected to the subject. The drawings and the recipes were published to announce the series of television programmes on Indian cookery. I thought the drawings on their own would not be enough. I asked Aparajita, my wife who has been spoiling me with culinary delights full of oriental and occidental promises since 1967, to write a few recipes to accompany the drawings.

In due course Jonathan teamed with Pené Prior, Sally Marks and Philip Demir produced 'A collector's book of eight delicious drawings by Biman Mullick accompanied by eight equally delicious recipes by Aparajita Mullick'. Truly a collector's item. Interestingly, this book represents four 'generations' of designers. I taught Jonathan, Jonathan taught Sally, and now Sally teaches Philip! As one can imagine, most of us are not collectors and it is not available to most of us. Therefore, Aparajita and I decided to produce an easily available edition of the book.

Here it is.

We both are grateful to Jonathan and his team.

I was a student at London's Saint Martin's School of Art from 1960 to 1964. At that time I discovered that a number of my teachers used to draw for Radio Times which had a tradition of publishing black and white drawings by well-known artists. I cherished the idea that one day I would draw for RT. It was in 1967 that I contacted RT and expressed my interest. In due course I was invited to show my drawings to the commissioning editor and to my delight one day I was asked to produce a drawing to announce a radio-play on a story from the Ramayana. The leading role was played by an unknown young actress called Judi Dench. The play was accompanied by music by Ravi Shankar. My experience of drawing for RT was challenging because of its deadline but it was highly rewarding. I remember those days and feel deeply nostalgic.

Biman Mullick

In India when I was young I used to watch my mum cooking. Sometimes I was allowed to help her between my 'home work'. Helping generally meant cutting vegetables, making dough for Rootis (Bengali Chapatis) and Luchis (Bengali Puris). My dad loved inviting friends and relatives and my mum used to produce a variety of wonderful tasty dishes. Now I cook from my memory. Whatever Biman, our daughter Sandra, our son-in-law James and our grand children, Olga Prothoma, Arthur Sobuj and Edith Mohima like to eat, I cook according to their taste. When I was in India, I remember that I learnt to cook a couple of dishes from my mum like cauliflower and potato curry; also I learnt how to fry Luchis. When I came to London, my mum used to send me recipes by post. For this project I had to write recipes, which is a completely new experience for me. Ordinarily, I cook without following recipes, a spontaneous exercise based on experience. I wanted to know if people would be able to follow my recipes and I immediately thought of my good friend Wiebke Thompson. She is seriously interested in foods of all kinds. Once she asked me to show her how to make Singaras. I showed her. The next day she made a few and brought some of them, fresh, crispy and hot, for us to taste. Biman and I were absolutely surprised. Biman commented, 'It tastes like Aparajita's.'

I asked her to try these recipes. She responded with great enthusiasm and cooked all eight dishes with excellent results.

We tasted them after she cooked them and were delighted that the recipes work.

Aparajita Mullick

In 1982, Biman Mullick was commissioned by Radio Times to produce a series of eight line-drawings to accompany a new series of programmes to be broadcast presenting Indian cuisine. The programme's chef was Madhur Jaffrey. Each drawing supported a single television programme and was greatly reduced to fit the narrow column page format of Radio Times. The drawings are much larger and printed here in their original size for the first time. Talk of producing this book has been the subject of many conversations between Biman and me for a number of years, but the stumbling block had been that only seven of the eight originals could be found. When the eighth was finally, and unexpectedly, unearthed by Aparajita, we could, at last, bring these drawings back to life.

Jonathan Doney

Tandoori, a tenderising treat

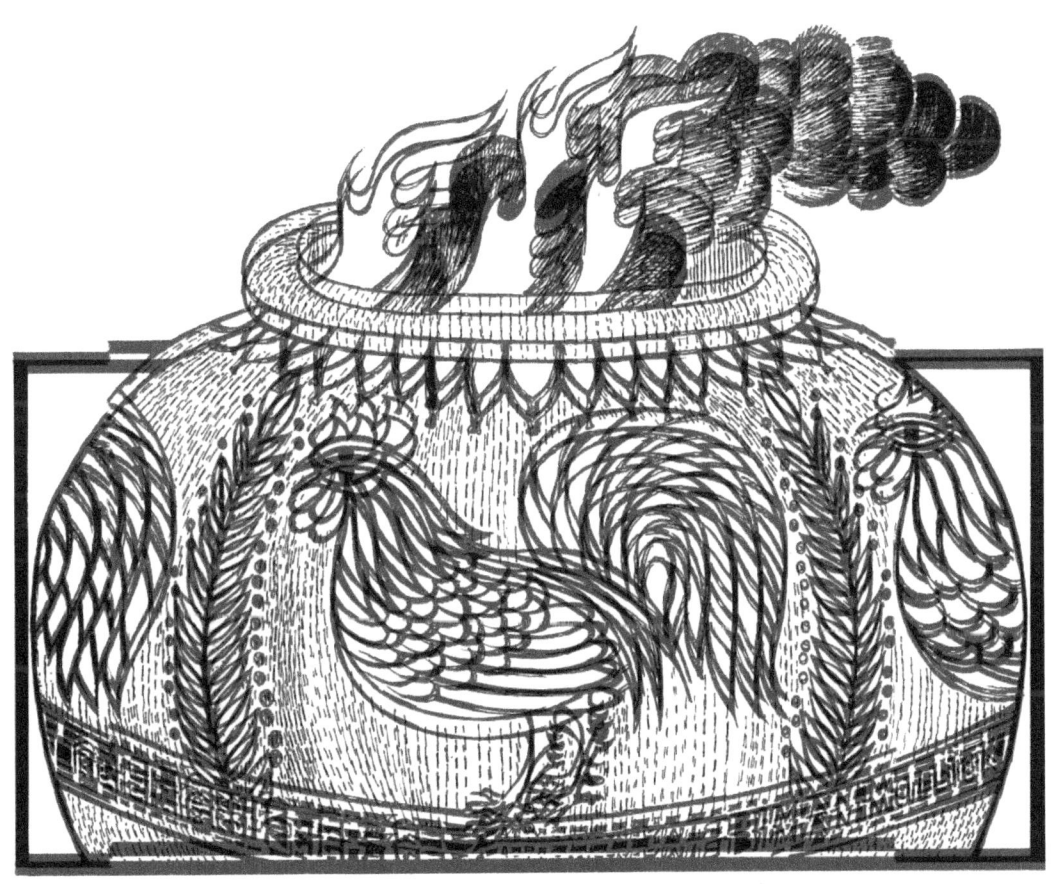

An Indian clay oven is called a Tandoor. This is not new information for present-day UK citizens. Wherever you reside in the UK, I am sure you will find a Tandoori restaurant. In the 60s and before, the word Tandoor was only known in Punjab and its surrounding areas. Chicken marinated in spices roasted in a clay oven buried underground was a speciality of this area. Now variations of this clay oven and Tandoori dishes are popular all over India. But the ovens are very rarely underground.

   Most households do not have this exotic kitchen gadget, but I find our common everyday gas or electric oven is a good alternative. Vegetables such as potatoes, onions, pumpkins and many more can be roasted with a blend of spices and are a welcome diversion from the traditional chicken.

This recipe serves 4 people as an accompaniment.
Preparation time: 30 minutes
Cooking time: 1 hour

Ingredients

4 medium potatoes peeled and cut into quarters
2 onions peeled and cut into thick slices for roasting
1 onion cut into small pieces for the sauce
1 inch of fresh ginger made into a paste (or finely chopped)
1 medium tomato, chopped
¼ teaspoon turmeric powder
⅛ teaspoon chilli powder
⅛ tablespoon sugar
Salt to taste
3 tablespoons rapeseed or sunflower oil

Method

1. Preheat the oven to gas mark 6 (200°C, 180°C fan).

2. Steam the potatoes for 12 minutes.

3. Fry the onions and add the turmeric powder, ginger, chilli powder, salt and sugar until light brown in colour.

4. Add the chopped tomatoes and cook for a further 10 minutes.

5. Mix the potatoes with the onions for roasting and coat them with the sauce made from the onions and spices.

6. Roast the mix for 30 minutes in the oven, gas mark 6 (200°C, 180°C fan)

Notes:

Aubergine, a virtuous vegetable

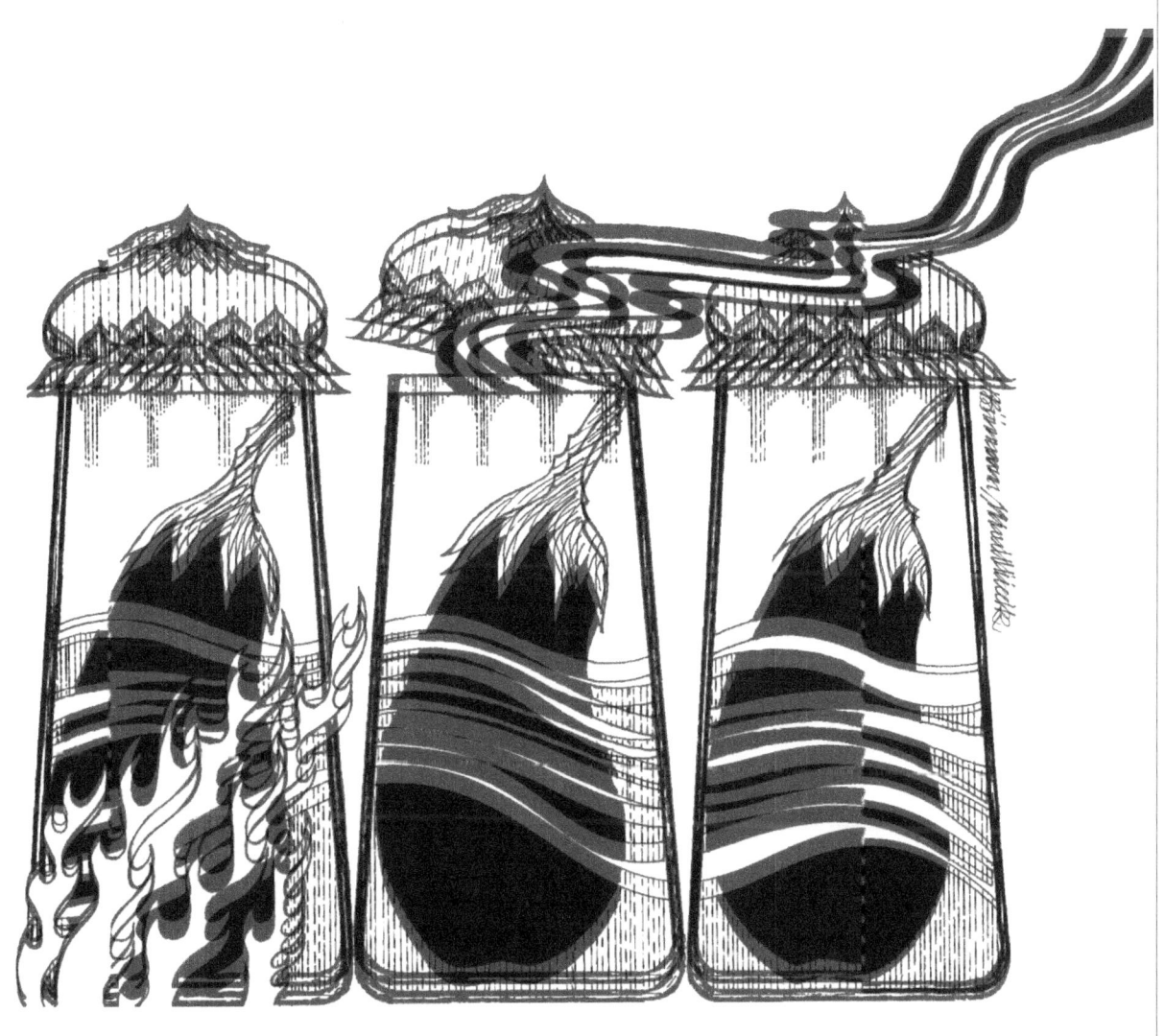

Aubergine has many different names such as Brinjal, Mad Apple, Melongene, Garden Egg, Guinea Squash and Eggplant. Its botanic name is *Solanum melongena*. In Sanskrit it is Bartaku. In Bengal it is known as Begoon, which is derived from the word Batingan. Unfortunately, the word Begoon (Be = without, goon = virtue) suggests that it is without virtue and without goodness. This is a total misunderstanding as in reality this is a versatile and delicious vegetable, which contains useful minerals such as potassium, phosphorus, magnesium, calcium, iron, sodium, manganese, copper and selenium.

Sprinkled with a little bit of salt, sugar and turmeric powder, aubergine can be simply shallow-fried using vegetable oil as 'Begoon Bhaja'; or Begoon can be deep-fried with gram flour (known as Besan) batter as 'Begooni'. As a healthy and delicious option it can be grilled and served (without burnt skin) with onion, ginger, green chilli, fresh coriander leaves and tomato as 'Begoon Pora' (Pora = Burnt) or 'Begoon Shneka' (Shneka = Lightly roasted or scorched). It is often fried with neem leaves, a favourite among Bengalis. Aubergine is one of the main ingredients of the famous 'Sookto', a bitter curry. It is also used in Ambal, a sour curry. In South India it is used in Sambar. The Greeks use aubergine in Moussaka. The French use it in Ratatouille. It is the main ingredient in Baba Ghanoush, a very popular dish in Turkey. It is also used in the famous dish called Hunkar Begendi, a luxurious lamb stew which is also known as 'Sultan's Delight'. In Bangladesh it is used in Bhorta. In the Middle East it is used in Imam Bayildi. The Chinese use aubergine in Di San Xian and other dishes. The versatility of aubergine is enormous.

Because of its high content of soft fibre, aubergine is good for the digestive system. Because it contains water it is also good for skin and hair. It can be used to control weight. To receive the full health benefit from an aubergine you should only use healthy recipes.

Here is one of my recipes for aubergine with tomato. It's healthy and tasty. Incidentally, in Bengal, a tomato is often referred to as a 'Bilati Begoon', meaning Begoon from London or a foreign Begoon. Therefore this preparation can be classified as fusion cuisine!

This recipe serves 4 people as an accompaniment.
Preparation time: 15 minutes
Cooking time: 30 minutes

Ingredients
1 medium aubergine
1 medium onion
4 tomatoes
⅛ teaspoon turmeric powder
⅛ teaspoon red chilli powder
Salt and sugar to taste
½ clove of garlic made into a paste
3 tablespoons rapeseed or sunflower oil

Method
1. Cut the aubergine into 2cm cubes.

2. Cut the onion into small pieces.

3. Shallow-fry the aubergine pieces in hot oil with salt and a little sugar.

4. Remove the fried aubergine and place in a separate bowl.

5. Fry the onion over a low heat for 10 minutes then add the garlic paste, turmeric powder, chilli powder, salt and ¼ teaspoon sugar and stir for a few minutes.

6. Add the chopped tomatoes. Cook for 10 minutes.

7. Add the fried aubergine to the tomato sauce and gently stir together.

Notes:

Biryani, with a conscience

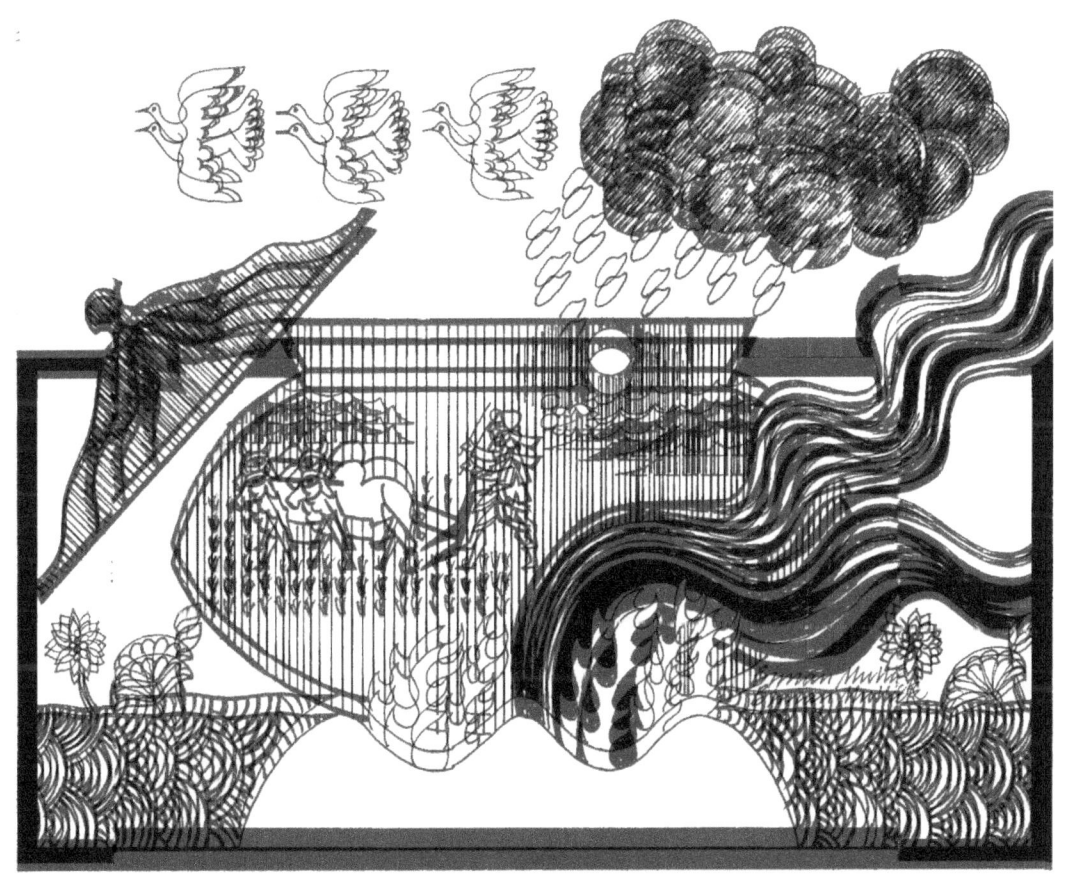

Traditionally, Biryani is a mixture of meat, rice, egg, yogurt and dried fruits. Most probably originated in Iraq and found its way to north Indian cuisine between 12th to 16th century. But so-called vegetable Biryani in many Indian restaurants in the UK are often left-over rice added to mixed vegetables straight from the tin served with an arbitrary choice of spices hurriedly prepared for the occasional vegetarian customer. These concoctions are always disappointing. Therefore, here is one I created.

**This recipe serves 4 people.
Preparation time: 1 hour
Cooking time: 1 hour 20 minutes**

Ingredients

4 tablespoons rapeseed or sunflower oil
4 medium onions (2 sliced and 2 cut into small pieces)
1 packet of 'Quorn'* chunks (300 g)
275 g Basmati rice
620 ml water for cooking the rice
1 pinch of saffron
½ teaspoon caraway seeds
4 cloves (finely ground)
4 whole cardamom pods (finely ground)
2 inches of cinnamon stick (finely ground)
(The cloves, cardamom and cinnamon can be ground together.)
3 garlic cloves (paste)
3 inches of ginger (paste)
3 green chillies (paste)

*'Quorn' is a trade name of a meat substitute and made from a 'mushroom'(Fusarium venenatum fungus). Paneer balls (recipe on page 39) can also be used instead of 'Quorn'.

(The garlic, ginger and chillies can be made into paste together with 3 tablespoons of water.)
260 g natural yoghurt
6 mint leaves
½ teaspoon ground nutmeg
4 whole almonds
6 pistachio nuts
(The almonds and pistachio nuts can be soaked over night, then peeled and sliced thinly.)
1 tablespoon Posto* (ground white poppy seeds)

*Posto (available from good Indian grocers) is actually opium poppy seeds but absolutely harmless. Often called Cus Cus or white poppy seeds, not to be confused with the wheat product called Couscous.

Method

1. Pre-heat the oven to gas mark 2 (150°C, 130°C fan).

2. Slice two onions and fry in two tablespoons of oil with a little salt and sugar.

3. Wash the rice and put it together with the 620 ml of water in a large pan. Bring to the boil and add a pinch of saffron. Cook over a low heat with the saucepan lid on until the rice is just cooked and the water has been absorbed.

4. Fry the other two onions (cut into small pieces) in two tablespoons of oil. When the onions are lightly browned, add the caraway seeds, ground cloves, cinnamon and cardamom mixture, the garlic, ginger and green chilli paste and ground Posto. Add the 'Quorn' and cook for a little while. 'Quorn' only needs cooking until it browns. Add salt and sugar according to taste.

5. In the bottom of a large casserole dish put a layer of rice, fried onion, the 'Quorn' mixture and yoghurt. Sprinkle a little nutmeg onto each layer. Repeat this several times according to the size of your casserole dish. Decorate the top layer with thinly sliced almonds and pistachio nuts, mint leaves and fried onion. Add a knob of butter to the top. Cover with a lid and cook in the pre-heated oven for 40 minutes.

Notes:

Rice can be mixed with different ingredients to make different dishes. One of them is khichuri. The great Kedgeree is derived from khichuri. Khichuri means mixture. A simple khichuri can be easily made with rice and any kind of lentil.

Protein in a pod

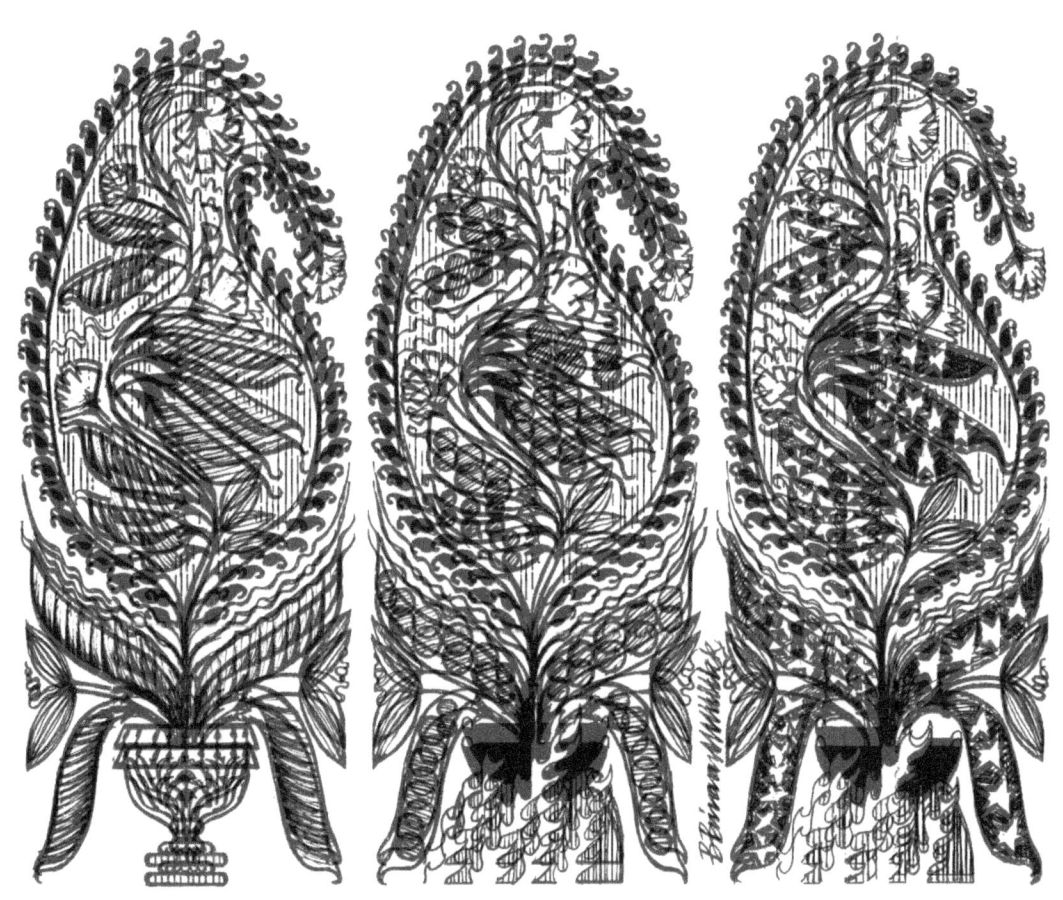

In the west, Indian cuisine generally refers to curry and curry is mostly associated with recipes involving meat. But most Indians are vegetarians and their main source of protein comes from various kinds of pulses. Of all the pulses, Musur Dal, the red lentil, is the most popular. If you order Dal in an Indian restaurant inevitably you will be served with Musur Dal. 'Dal Bhat', lentils and boiled rice, is the 'bread and butter' of Indians. It is also one of the easiest to prepare. It is the most balanced mixture of carbohydrate and protein, and also one of the least expensive dishes in the list of Indian food items. Naturally, 'Dal Bhat' is a very popular food combination in India.

Serves 3 or 4 people as an accompaniment.
Preparation time: 30 minutes
Cooking time: 20 minutes

Ingredients

500 ml water
170 g of husked and split Moong Dal
¼ teaspoon turmeric powder
2 bay leaves
2 pieces of peeled, fresh ginger, made into a paste using a blender or pestle & mortar. Half of it to be boiled with the Dal and the other half to be added while frying.
1 tablespoon rapeseed or sunflower oil
1 teaspoon whole cumin seeds
1 green chilli, thinly chopped
1 teaspoon dry-roasted whole cumin seeds (ground)
½ teaspoon sugar
3 tablespoons frozen peas
Salt to taste to be added at the end.

Method

1. Boil the Moong Dal with turmeric powder, bay leaves, and crushed ginger for 25 minutes until the Dal is soft.

2. Heat the oil in a saucepan, add whole cumin seeds, ginger paste, thinly chopped green chilli, ground roasted cumin seeds and sugar and cook for 10 seconds approx., then add the boiled Dal.

3. Steam the handful of frozen peas in the Dal before serving.

Serve with freshly cooked Basmati rice and any curry of your choice.

Notes:

Charismatic Korma

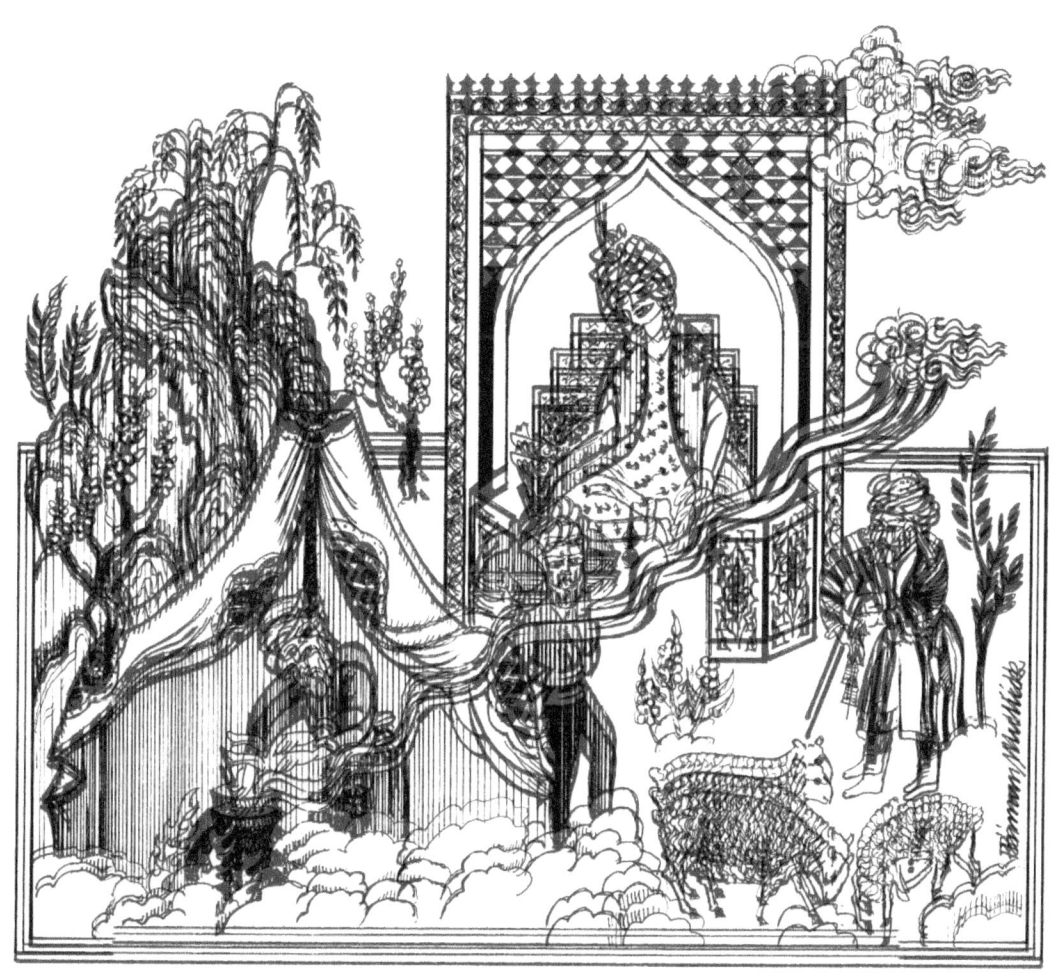

If you ask for Korma in an Indian restaurant, most probably you will be served with pieces of roast chicken covered with a sickly and insipid sweet sauce. This is far from what you would expect in an Indian household. Korma is a mild curry with a distinct flavour. The original recipe most probably came to India from Turkey via Persia and the mildness comes from nuts such as coconut, almonds and cashews.

This recipe serves 3 people. Preparation and cooking time: 2 hours

Ingredients

- 5 tablespoons rapeseed or sunflower oil
- ½ teaspoon turmeric powder
- 50 g ground almonds soaked in 200 ml of milk
- Half a butternut squash
- Half a cauliflower cut into small pieces
- 3 tablespoons frozen green peas
- Quarter of a red pepper, cut into small pieces
- 2 garlic cloves made into a paste
- 2 inches of ginger made into a paste
- 2 or 3 green chillies cut into very small pieces or made into a paste
- 1 tablespoon dry roasted almond flakes

(Please note that ground almonds can be substituted with single cream. The result would be different but quite acceptable.)

Method

1. Pre-heat the oven to gas mark 5 (190°C, 170°C fan).

2. Peel and cut the butternut squash into small cubes. Coat with one tablespoon of oil and a little salt and sugar.

3. Roast the butternut squash in the oven for 25 to 30 minutes until cooked.

4. Steam the frozen green peas and keep in a bowl when cooked.

5. Shallow-fry the cauliflower pieces in the heated oil with a little of the turmeric powder, salt and sugar, a little ginger paste and a little green chilli paste.

6. Put the lid on and cook for 5 minutes with a little water or until the cauliflower is cooked. In this way, less oil will be absorbed by the cauliflower. Keep the fried cauliflower pieces in a bowl when cooked.

7. Put the remaining ginger, chilli and garlic paste, ½ teaspoon of turmeric powder, sugar and salt to taste in hot oil in a frying pan. Cook for 4 minutes.

8. Add the almond and milk mixture. Cook for 5 minutes.

9. Add the roasted butternut squash and the fried cauliflower and boil for another 10 minutes.

10. Add the green peas right at the end and decorate with the red pepper pieces and dry roasted almond flakes.

Serve with rice or Chapatis.

Notes:

Singara, horns without dilemmas

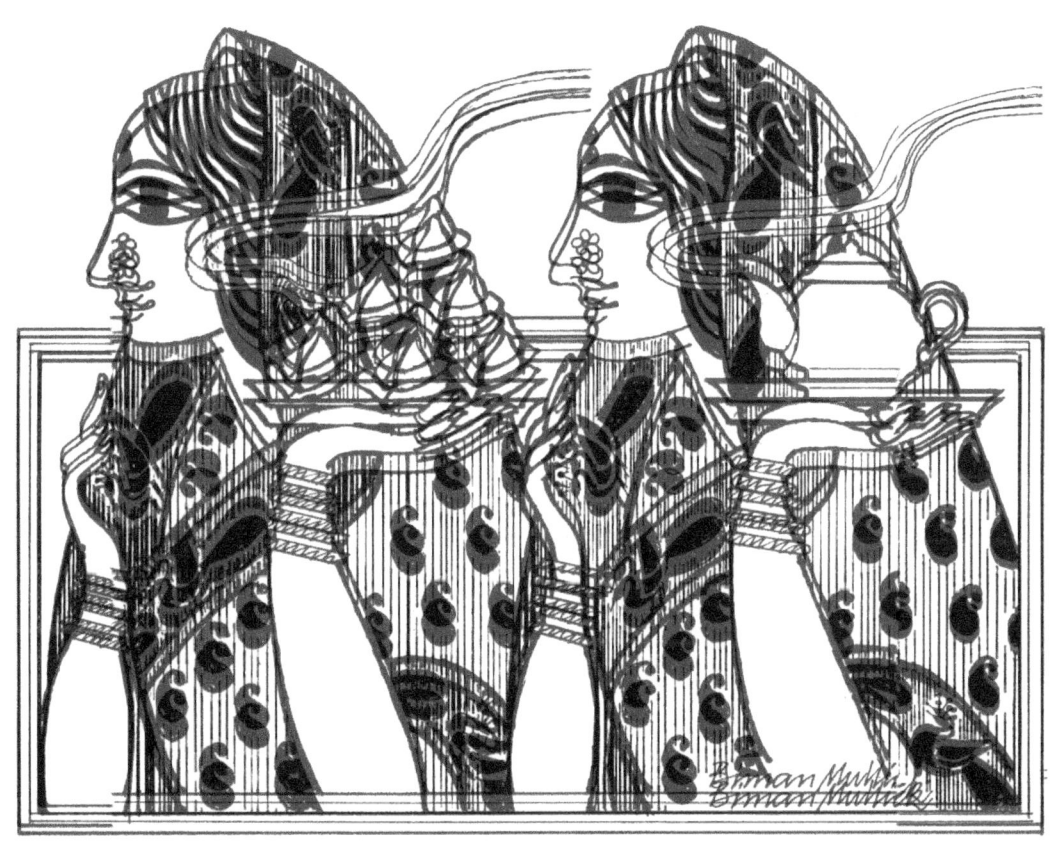

The Bengali word Singara has nothing to do with the ancient Mesopotamian port called Singara. It refers to triangular-shaped Bengali snacks. The word 'Singara' came from the Sanskrit word 'Sringatak', meaning something with 'sringa', that is to say a horn or horns. Technically anything from an ill-tempered rhino to an innocent paniphal (a kind of water chestnut, *Trapa natans*), including mighty Rudolf the reindeer, all are 'Singaras'. Variations of Bengali Singaras are found all over the world under slightly different names and with different fillings, such as Ethiopian Sambusa, Greek Tiropeta and Argentinian Empanadas. In the west Singaras are known by their Hindi name, Samosas.

Here is my recipe for Singara.

This recipe makes 16 Singaras.
Preparation and cooking time: 2 hours

Ingredients

For the dough:
250 g plain flour
4 tablespoons rapeseed or sunflower oil
½ teaspoon salt
20 fluid oz cold water

For the stuffing:
4 peeled potatoes
Quarter of a cauliflower cut into small florets
60 g frozen green peas
1 inch of fresh peeled ginger made into a paste
Salt and sugar to taste
2 teaspoons dry roasted ground cumin seeds
Red chilli powder to taste
Garam masala (clove, cardamom and cinnamon ground together.)

For frying:
Rapeseed or sunflower oil or Ghee (divinely delicious but not good for your heart.)

Method

1. Make the dough with cold water. Knead for 10 minutes. After making the dough keep it for 1 hour in a warm room, not in the fridge.

2. Peel the potatoes, cut them into small 1 cm cubes and steam until cooked.

3. Steam the frozen green peas until cooked.

4. Fry the small cauliflower florets with 1 inch of fresh ginger (made into paste) with salt and sugar. Add two teaspoons of dry roasted ground cumin seeds, red chilli powder and garam masala.

5. Make eight similar balls of pastry. Roll them in oval shapes roughly eight inches long. Cut each in half. Then make a cone shape. Brush water inside and on the opposite flap. Fold the flap over and press.

6. Put a little of the stuffing in the cone shape and close.

7. Deep-fry each of the Singaras slowly in the oil over a low heat for 5 to 10 minutes until golden brown.

Notes:

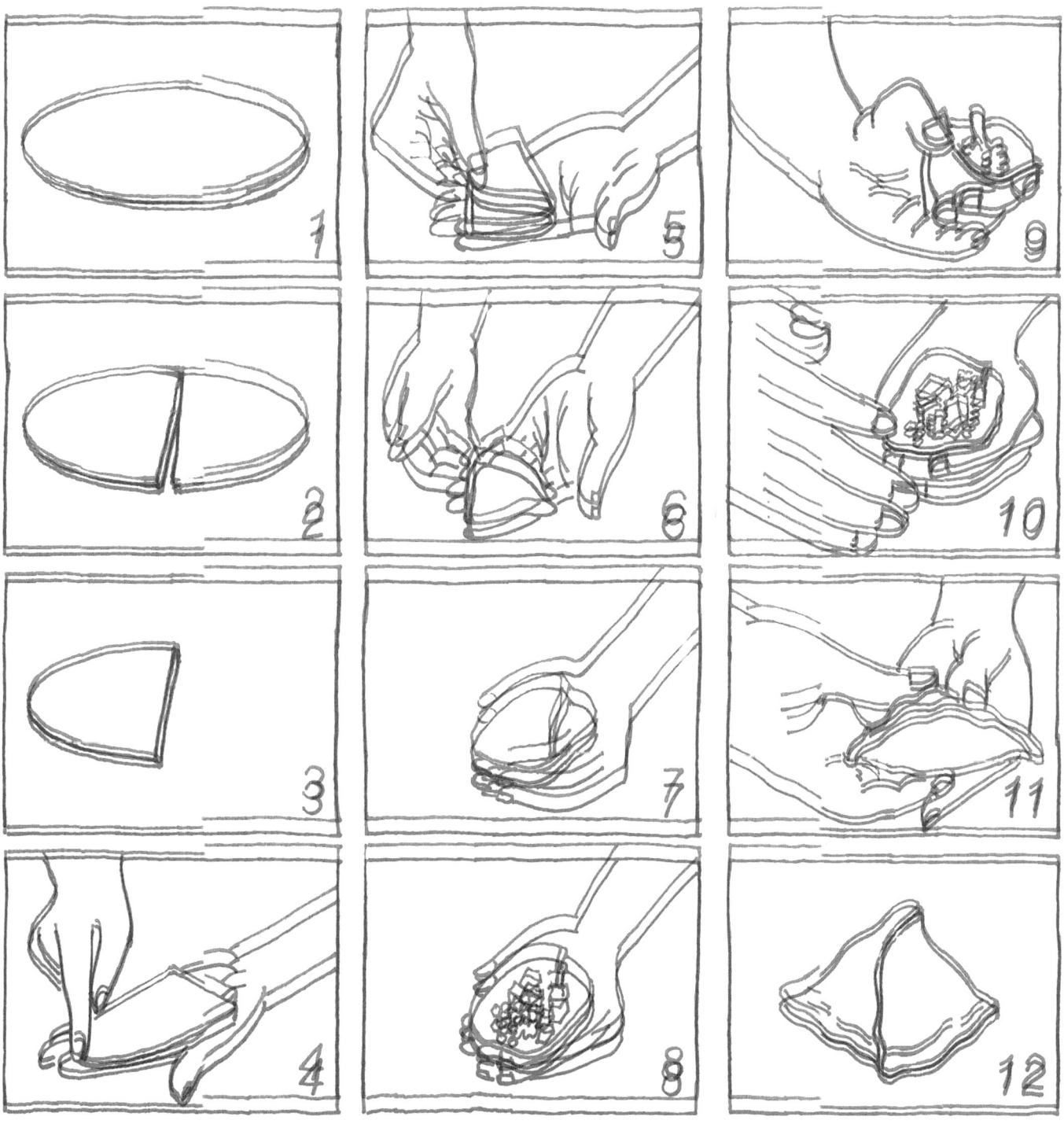

A different ball game

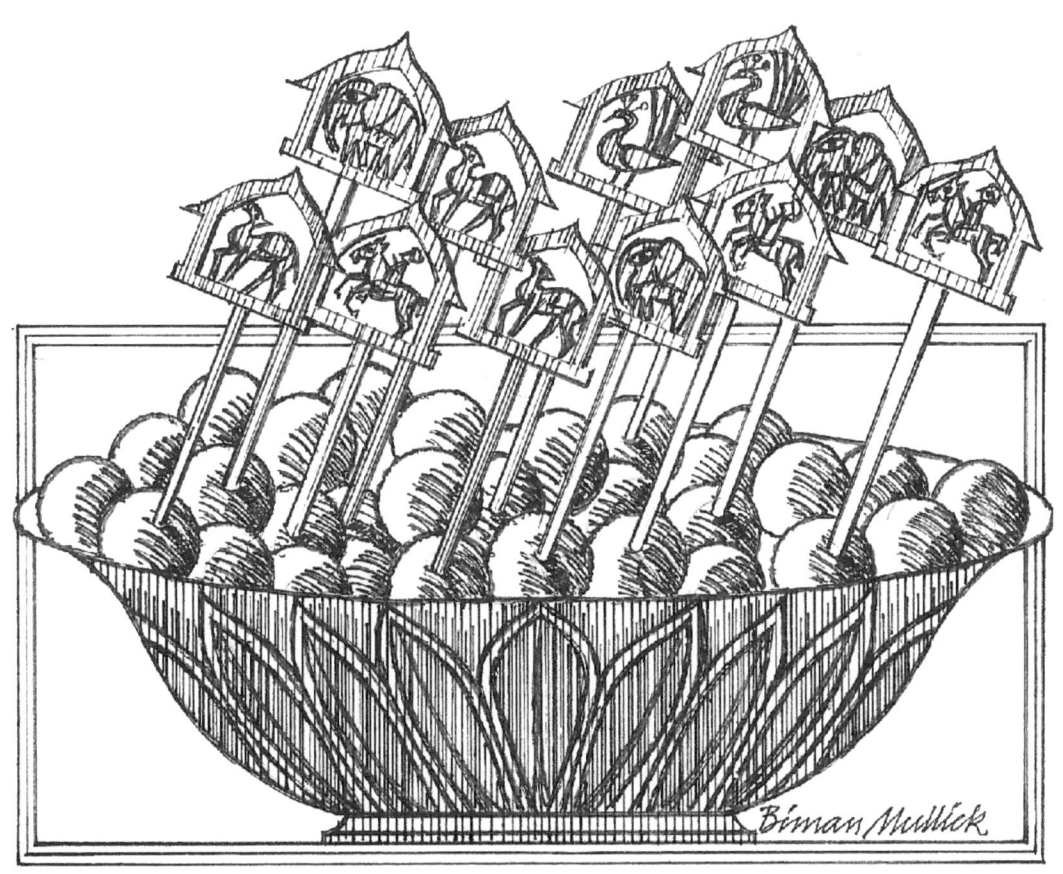

Traditionally an English afternoon tea generally consists of sandwiches, scones, biscuits, cakes and pastries with accompaniments such as cream and jam. But traditional Indian (Bengali) afternoon tea quite often includes spicy savoury dishes such as Chanachur, Pakoras, Singaras, Kochuris and Nimkis along with sweets such as Sandesh, Barphis, Rosogollas, Pantuas and Jilipis. They are more than nibbles, they are more serious snacks for all seasons and all occasions! They are also common at all festive occasions as pre-dinner starters and served in informal social gatherings and parties. Here is my own addition to this group of dishes for a casual mealtime.

This recipe makes 12 Paneer balls (spicy Chhana balls).
Preparation time: 4 hours
Cooking time: 30 minutes

Ingredients

4 pints whole milk
Juice of 1 lemon
1 inch of ginger made into a paste
½ teaspoon dry-roasted Jeera (cumin) powder
Pinch of salt to taste
10 tablespoons rapeseed or sunflower oil for deep-frying
Little bit of plain flour to coat the Paneer balls

Method

1: Boil the milk.

2: Add the lemon juice when the milk has boiled.

3: Turn the heat off.

4: The milk will start to curdle and separates into greenish-coloured water (whey) and Paneer.

5: Drain the Paneer (Chhana-Cheese). Put it in muslin or a big strainer. Leave it to drain the water for at least 3 hours.

6: Put the Paneer in the blender, add the ginger paste, dry-roasted Jeera and a little bit of salt to taste.

7: Make 12 balls and coat with a little bit of plain flour.

8: Deep-fry the Paneer balls. Turn the balls very carefully when one side is slightly brown.

9: Place the cooked Paneer balls on kitchen paper to cool.

Notes:

These are a great addition to Biriyani, recipe page 30.

A roast to grace your table

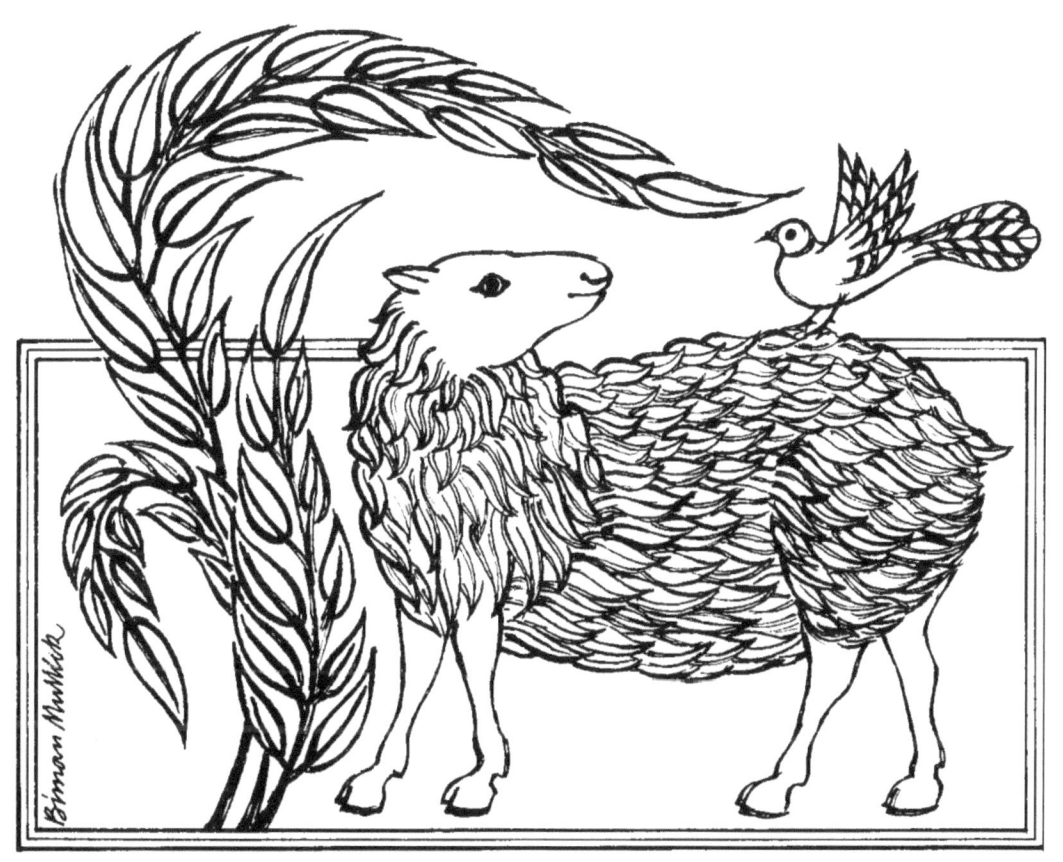

Most Indian kitchens do not have an oven of the type we have here in the west. Therefore, no roasting, even on a Sunday, takes place in an Indian household. Most Indians are also vegetarian. Here, I took full advantage of our domestic oven and created a completely new type of simple 'Indian' dish using easily available vegetables and a few spices to add a bit of flavour and a bit of extra taste. I have chosen an uncommon combination of a few spices which enhances the taste of the vegetables without losing their original colour, texture, flavour and taste. I hope this roast not only graces your dining table but also tickles your taste buds!

This recipe serves 4 people as an accompaniment:
Preparation time: 30 minutes
Cooking time: 35 minutes

Ingredients

1 red pepper
1 green pepper
1 yellow pepper
2 red onions
2 sweet potatoes
2 courgettes
3 inches of ground cinnamon stick
3 teaspoons coarsely ground coriander
½ teaspoon chilli powder
3 tablespoons rapeseed or sunflower oil
1 tablespoon sugar
Salt to taste

Method

1. Pre-heat the oven to gas mark 6 (200°C, 180°C fan).

2. Cut the courgettes into 1x2cm pieces.

3. Peel the sweet potatoes then cut into 1x2cm pieces.

4. Slice the red, yellow and green peppers lengthwise into 1x2cm pieces.

5. Cut the red onion into thick slices.

6. Fry the red, yellow and green peppers and the onion with salt, sugar, ground coriander, chilli powder and ground cinnamon for 5 minutes to coat the vegetables with spices and hot oil.

7. After frying a little, put them in a roasting tin and place this in the oven.

8. Fry the courgettes and sweet potatoes with all the spices and put them in a separate roasting tin and place this in the oven.

9. After 20 minutes check and turn the vegetables

10. Roast both tins for a total of 35 minutes at gas mark 6 (200°C, 180°C fan).

Notes:

Biman Mullick is a London-based artist, social activist and marathon runner. Born in Howrah, West Bengal, in 1933, he moved to London in 1960 and studied at Saint Martin's School of Art. In 1969, he designed the Gandhi centenary commemorative stamp for the Royal Mail, the first stamp to be designed by an overseas artist. In 1971, he designed the first set of eight stamps issued by the newly formed Republic of Bangladesh. He has received awards from the World Health Organisation, the Republic of Bangladesh and Bangladesh citizens in the UK. He has also taught at several institutions including Middlesex University and Kingston University. His work is published in numerous books and journals. At present he is engaged in producing picture books especially for children who are learning in a non-Bengali environment. He and his wife, Aparajita, have been married since 1967.

Aparajita Mullick studied science at Serampore College, West Bengal, India, and received a Bachelor of Science degree from the University of Burdwan. Since moving to London with Biman in 1967 she has worked as a laboratory technician in a comprehensive school, computer operator in a further education college and export buyer at the Crown Agents, UK. Aparajita enjoys keeping fit by practising yoga and tai chi, loves gardening, travelling, taking photographs and of course cooking, especially with her three grandchildren.

Jonathon Doney was taught typography and graphic design by Biman Mullick and Ivan Cooper during the late 1960s at Harlow Technical College. Since then, Jonathon has had a successful and award-winning career as a typographer, book designer and teacher; and establishing The Spitfire Press in 2000 producing limited edition letterpress print work. He is a Fellow of the International Society of Typographic Designers and was its Chair from 2004 to 2009.

Notes:

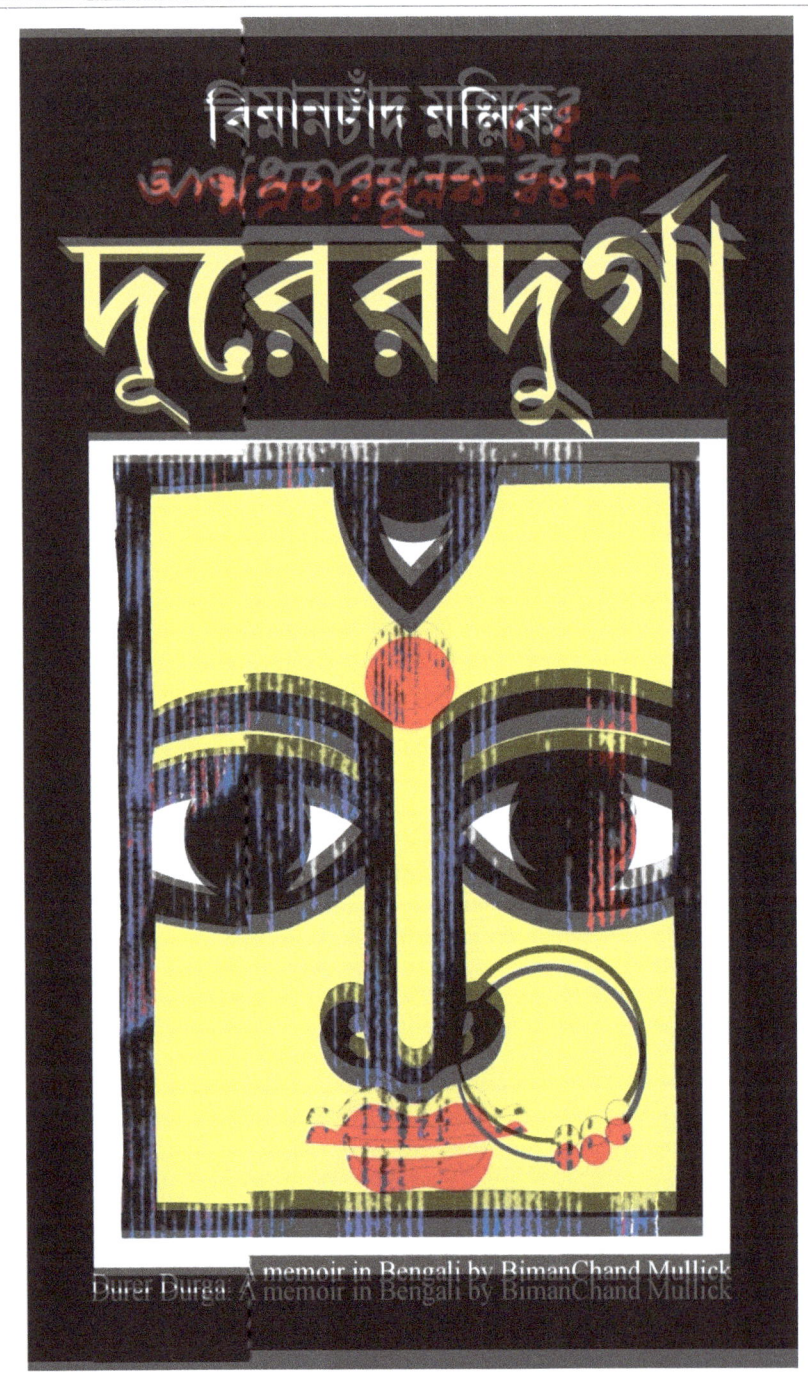

Durer Durga: Distant Durga
A memoir in Bengali
by BimanChand Mullick

'...wonderful mixture of history and experience; deliciously enjoyable.'
Juthika Banerjee: London ☙

'It is like enjoying your story in the living room.' Soma Choudhury: USA ☙

'...delightful memoir... at times hilarious.'
S N Sanyal: Chandigar ☙

'I believe, the pictorial index is an unusual introduction in the field of book design.'
John Dalley, a book designer ☙

'আধুনিক বাংলা সাহিত্যের তালিকায় একটি উল্লেখযোগ্য সংযোজন।' আব্দুল মতিন: লন্ডন ☙

'অসাধারণ, অসাধারণ সুন্দর।' ভবন বাংচী: ঢাকা ☙

'স্মৃতিকথার সঙ্গে দুইদেশের ইতিহাস; বৈশিষ্ট্য রসিকতায়।' উইলিয়াম রাদিচে: YouTube ☙

'ভাবছি আপনি তো কেবল লিখতেই পারেন, অথবা সৈয়দ মুজতবা আলীর মত।'
সন্ধিতা: ঢাকা ☙

International edition
ISBN 9781534937987
is available on the Internet from
Amazon
All-colour Paperback
£ 13.93 / US $ 31.00

Indian edition
ISBN 978-81-938332-0-9
is available from
Thema
46 Satish Mukherjee Road
Kolkata 700026
Phone: +91 8420124541
+913324667794
Email themabooks@yahoo.com
All-colour Hardback: Rs. 650.00

My 1st Book of Bengali by Biman Mullick

This highly colourful picture book is mainly produced for English-speaking children to have fun with pictures and words using Roman and Bengali alphabets. It should encourage them to learn and appreciate the Bengali language. Though most of the book can be followed without prior knowledge of Bengali, it helps if someone with a good knowledge of the language can guide young readers. This is not a comprehensive 'Teach yourself Bengali' but a pre-school picture book of fun. Originally it was created for Olga Prothoma, Arthur Sobul and Edith Mohima by their Dadu the grandfather. Now it is made available for all children. Interested adults can have fun as well.

ISBN 9781839142744 Available on the Internet through Amazon

From My 1st Book of Bengali:

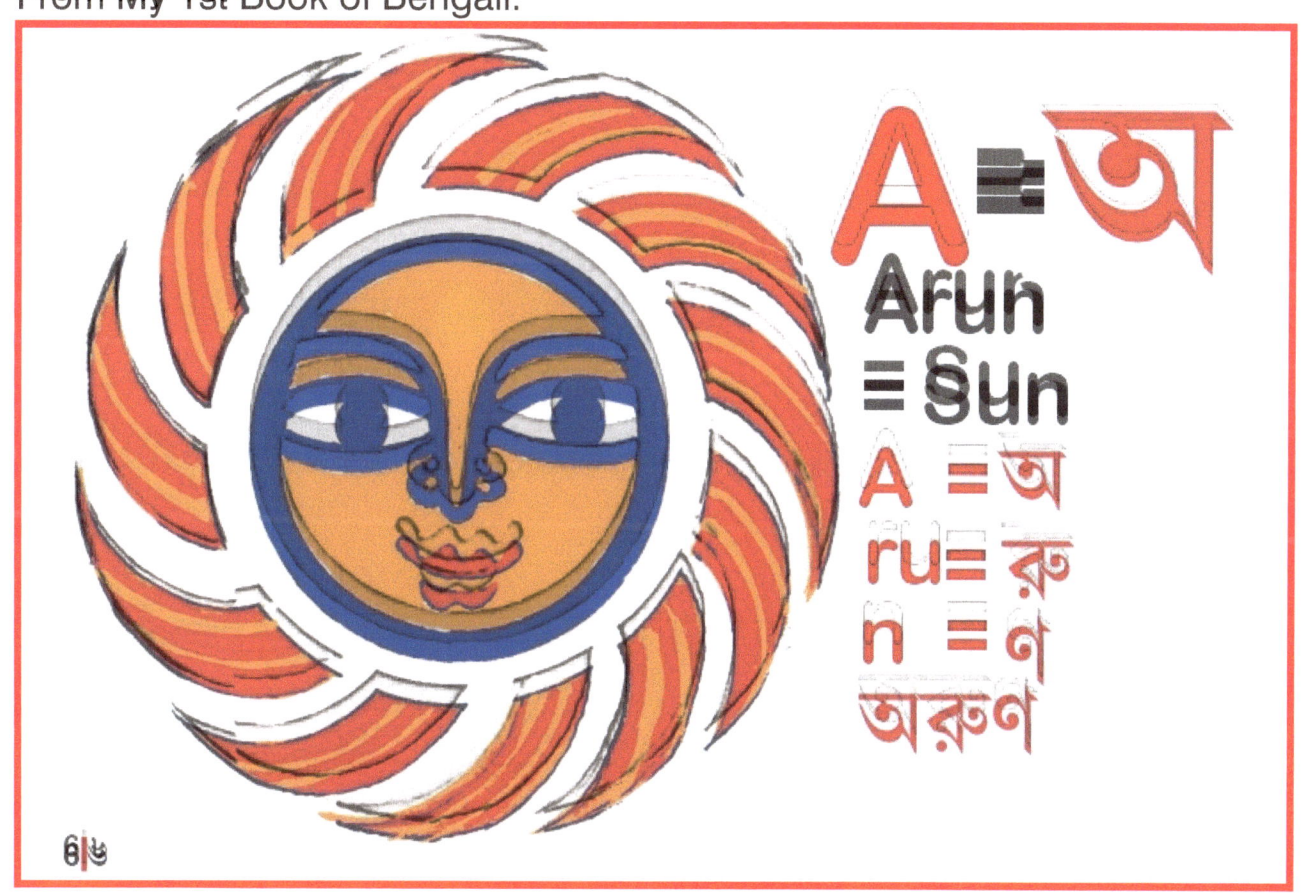

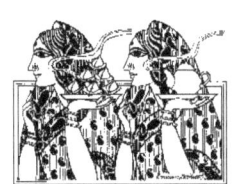

The end

www.ingramcontent.com/pod-product-compliance
Lightning Source LLC
Chambersburg PA
CBHW051926210526
45473CB00006B/2149